ZAKYNTHOS

TRAVEL GUIDE 2025

Discovering Zakynthos Culture Cuisine Hidden Gems Thrilling and Local Insights

Parson Reames

COPYRIGHT

© 2025 [Parson Reames]. All rights reserved.

This book is protected under copyright law and may not be reproduced, distributed, or shared in any form or by any means—whether electronic, mechanical, photocopying, recording, or otherwise—without the express written consent of the copyright holder, unless it is for brief quotations used in reviews or academic works.

The content in this guide is provided for general informational purposes. While every effort has been made to ensure the information is accurate, the author and publisher are not liable for any errors, omissions, or changes in the content.

CONTENT

INTRODUCTION TO ZAKYNTHOS 9
History of Zakynthos 11
Geography And Climate 13
The People And Culture 14
10 Best Reasons To Visit Zakynthos 15
Dons And Donts 18

ESSENTIAL PLANNING 20
Best Time To Visit 20
Visa And Tavelling Documents 21
Packing List And Useful Apps 23
Currency And Banking 25
SIM Cards And Internet 27
Health And Safety Information 30
Emergency Contacts And Resources 31
Local Etiquette In Zakynthos 33

TRANSPORTATION OPTIONS 35
Getting There 35
Ferry Options 37
Public Transport 40
Renting A Car, Scooter And Boat 42

  Water Taxis And Island Hopping 43
  Tips For Renting A Car In Zakynthos 45
ACCOMMODATION 47
  Luxury Hotels And Resorts 47
  Hostels And Guesthouses 49
  Family -Friendly Stays And Hostels 50
  Choosing The Right Accomodations 52
REGIONS ATTRACTIONS 54
  Navagio Beach 54
  Blue Caves 58
  Askos Stone Park 60
  Keri Cliffs And Lighthouse 61
  Marathonisi (Turtle Island) 63
  Bohali Hill 65
  Solomos Square And Zakynthos Town 67
  Zakynthos' Villages 70
ZAKYNTHIAN CUISINE 72
  Traditional Cuisine 72
  Must-Try Dishes And Street Food 73
  Top Restaurants, Cafés, And Dining Spots 75
  Zakynthian Wines And Vineyards 76
  Local Crafts And Handicrafts 77
ZAKYNTHIAN CULTURAL EXPERIENCES 79

Traditional Festivals And Cultural Events 79
Churches And Monasteries 80
Tops Museums 81
Historical And Cultural Landmarks 82
Attractions For Kids 84
Parks And Garden 85
Top Beaches 86
Interacting with Locals 87

NIGHTLIFE AND ENTERTAINMENT 89
Clubs And Bars 89
Casinos And Local Breweries 90
Family-Friendly Nightlife Options 91
Evening Entertainment 92
Tips For A Safe And Fun Night Out 93

OUTDOOR ACTIVITIES AND ADVENTURES 94
Boat Trips 94
Snorkeling And Diving 96
Watersports 97
Blue Caves Exploration 98
Turtle Spotting 99
Porto Limnionas Swimming 100

SHOPPING, AND SPAS 102

Gifts Ideas 102
Local And Modern Markets 103
Luxury Boutique And Malls 104
Spa And Wellness Retreats 105
Traditional Healing And Massage 106
Tips for Shopping Responsibly 107
ITINERARIES SUGGESTIONS 109
4 Days Beach And Watersports Itinerary 109
7 Days Family Friendly Itinerary 111
5 Days Curlinary Itenarary 113
CONCLUSION 117

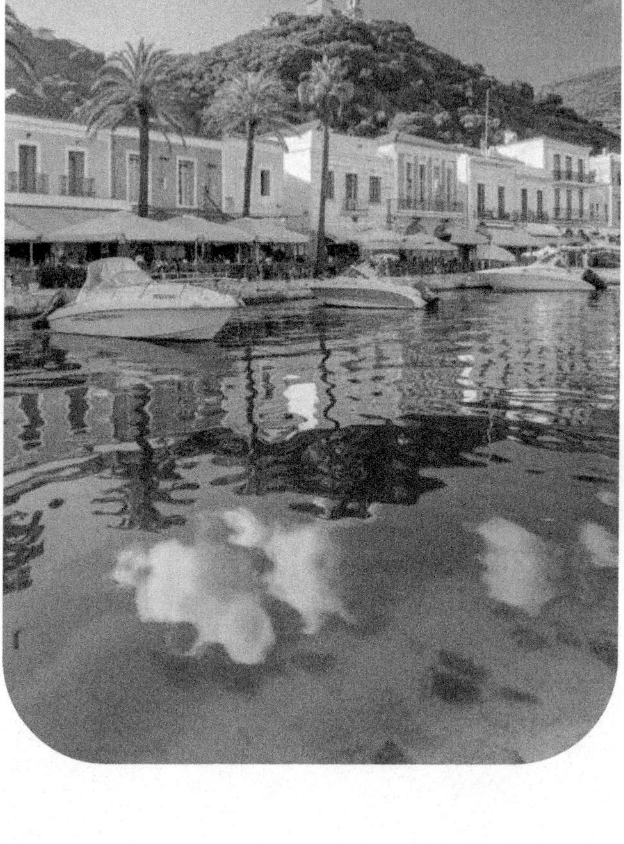

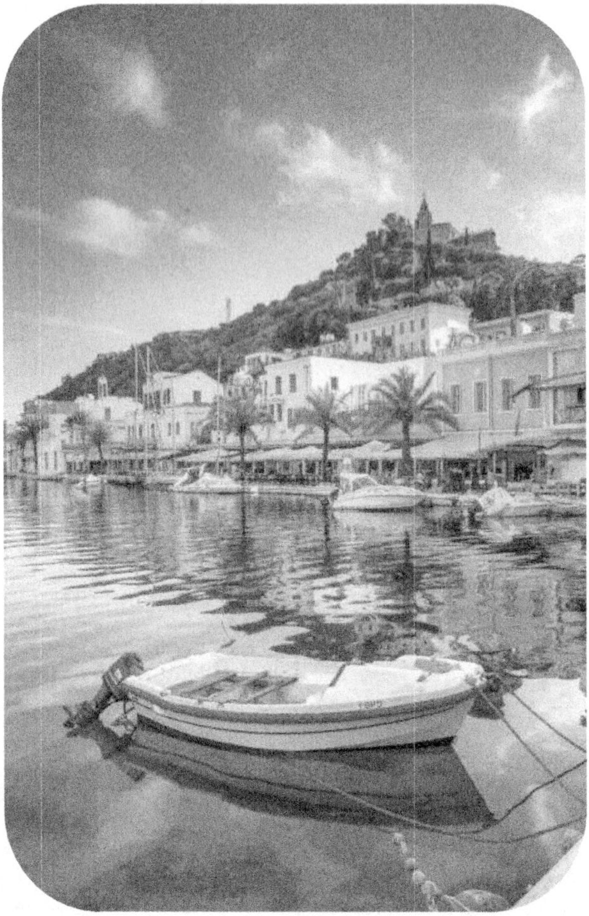

INTRODUCTION TO ZAKYNTHOS

Zakynthos, the southernmost of the Ionian Islands, is a place where rugged cliffs meet electric-blue waters, olive groves stretch as far as the eye can see, and life moves to the rhythm of the waves. It's the kind of destination that sticks with you long after you've left, whether it's the image of the sun setting over the Ionian Sea, the taste of fresh seafood in a waterfront taverna, or the feeling of warm sand underfoot on one of its postcard-perfect beaches.

This island has a reputation that precedes it, thanks to the world-famous Navagio Beach. That iconic cove, with its rusting shipwreck stranded on blinding white pebbles, is the kind of place you expect to see on a travel brochure. But Zakynthos isn't just a one-hit wonder. Beyond the shipwreck, you'll find limestone caves carved by the sea, mountain villages where time seems to slow down, and a coastline so diverse that you can swim in a different setting every day hidden coves, sweeping sandy bays, and rocky inlets where the water is impossibly clear.

It's an island that feels both lively and untouched at the same time. The southern coast, particularly around Laganas, has long drawn travelers looking for nightlife, while the western cliffs and northern shores remain wild and dramatic. Inland, Zakynthos is a patchwork of vineyards, citrus groves, and sleepy hamlets, a side of the island that's often overlooked but offers some of its most authentic experiences. Nature lovers have plenty to get excited about. Zakynthos is one of the last strongholds of the endangered loggerhead sea turtle, and the National Marine Park of Zakynthos protects both the turtles and the unspoiled beaches they nest on. You can take a boat trip to watch them swim in the turquoise waters of Laganas Bay or simply spend time on beaches like Gerakas, where conservation efforts mean sharing the sand with these ancient creatures. The island's limestone cliffs and sea caves add to the adventure, whether you're kayaking through natural rock arches or diving into underwater caverns.

The food here is an experience in itself. Zakynthian cuisine leans heavily on fresh, local ingredients, with olive oil that's as much a part of daily life as the sea breeze. Traditional tavernas serve slow-cooked lamb, spicy cheeses, and seafood plucked straight from the water, best enjoyed with a glass of Verdea, the island's distinctive white wine. Zakynthos is more than a summer escape; it's a place with a rhythm all its own. Whether you're here for the beaches, the nightlife, or the quiet charm of its villages, the island has a way of pulling you in. The hardest part isn't getting here it's leaving.

History of Zakynthos

Zakynthos, or Zante, has a history as captivating as its landscapes, shaped by centuries of conquests, cultural influences, and resilience. The island's story stretches back to antiquity, named after Zakynthos, the son of Arcadian chief Dardanus. Its strategic location in the Ionian Sea made it a valuable prize for various civilizations, each leaving behind traces of their presence. The Mycenaeans were among the first settlers, followed by the Romans, who introduced architectural advancements and trade networks.

During the Byzantine era, Zakynthos flourished as a cultural and commercial hub, with churches and monasteries dotting the landscape. This period cemented the island's role as a crossroads between East and West. The Venetian rule, which began in the late 15th century, brought prosperity and a distinctive architectural and artistic influence. Zakynthos Town still bears traces of this era, from grand mansions to fortifications, while Venetian traditions also shaped local music and cuisine. The island's role in Greece's struggle for independence in the 19th century was significant, with many locals actively joining the fight against Ottoman rule. Monuments and museums commemorate their contributions. However, Zakynthos faced immense challenges in the 20th century, particularly the devastating earthquakes of 1953, which reduced much of the island to rubble. Despite this, the Zakynthians rebuilt, preserving their cultural heritage while embracing modern development.

Today, Zakynthos is a thriving tourist destination, known for its stunning beaches, crystalline waters, and lively atmosphere. Yet, beyond its natural beauty, the island's rich history is ever-present, whether in the remnants of ancient settlements, Venetian squares, or the traditions passed down through generations. Zakynthos is more than just a summer retreat it's an island with a soul shaped by centuries of triumphs and challenges.

Geography And Climate

Zakynthos, the third-largest Ionian Island, covers 405 square kilometers with a coastline stretching 123 kilometers. The eastern region is fertile, with olive groves, vineyards, and citrus orchards, while the western side is rugged, featuring dramatic cliffs and Mount Vrachionas, the highest peak at 758 meters. The island is home to stunning beaches, each offering a unique experience. Navagio Beach, with its iconic shipwreck, is the most famous, while Laganas, Gerakas, and Porto Limnionas attract visitors with their crystal-clear waters and scenic beauty. Zakynthos' varied terrain makes it a paradise for nature lovers, offering breathtaking coastal and mountainous landscapes.

Climate of Zakynthos

Zakynthos enjoys a Mediterranean climate, bringing hot, dry summers and mild, wet winters. Summers see temperatures between 25°C and 30°C, with July and August often exceeding 30°C. Winters are cooler but rarely drop below 5°C, with most rainfall occurring between December and February. Spring and autumn offer comfortable weather, making them ideal for outdoor exploration and avoiding summer crowds. The island's climate, moderated by the Ionian Sea, keeps the landscape lush and green throughout the year. Whether basking in summer sun or enjoying mild off-season weather, Zakynthos provides excellent conditions for visitors in every season.

The People And Culture

Zakynthos is an island where tradition and modern life blend seamlessly. The Zakynthians are known for their hospitality, strong sense of heritage, and passion for music, food, and celebration. Influenced by Venetian, French, and British rule, the island's culture is a unique mix reflected in its architecture, cuisine, and customs. Music and dance are integral to Zakynthian life. Traditional folk music, accompanied by bouzouki and mandolin, fills festivals and gatherings, while the island's choral traditions add a distinct touch to both religious and secular events. Dancing is equally important, with locals enthusiastically performing syrtos and kalamatianos at celebrations.

Zakynthian cuisine is deeply rooted in Mediterranean flavors, relying on fresh, local ingredients. Olive oil, wine, and honey are at the heart of many dishes. Signature specialties include sartsa, a beef stew with tomatoes and cheese, *skordostoumbi*, a garlicky eggplant dish, and *ladotyri*, a cheese preserved in olive oil. Meals are a social experience, often enjoyed with family and friends. Religion plays a vital role in daily life, with numerous historic churches and monasteries across the island. The most significant religious event is the feast of Saint Dionysios, celebrated with grand processions and festivities on August 24th and December 17th, drawing both locals and visitors.

Zakynthians also have a deep appreciation for their island's natural beauty. From hiking in the hills to swimming in crystal-clear waters, outdoor activities are a way of life. The island's breathtaking landscapes provide endless opportunities for exploration. Warm, welcoming, and deeply connected to their traditions, the people of Zakynthos embody the island's spirit. Whether through food, music, or nature, their vibrant culture creates an atmosphere that leaves a lasting impression on visitors.

10 Best Reasons To Visit Zakynthos

Navagio Beach (Shipwreck Beach); One of the most famous beaches in Greece, Navagio Beach is a breathtaking sight with its striking white cliffs, crystal-clear waters, and the iconic shipwreck resting on the sand. Accessible only by boat, this secluded cove offers an unforgettable experience and is a must-visit spot for travelers.

The Blue Caves; Located along the northern coast, the Blue Caves are a mesmerizing natural wonder. The sunlight reflecting off the water creates stunning shades of blue, giving the caves a magical glow. The best way to explore them is by boat, with opportunities to swim in the vibrant waters.

Loggerhead Sea Turtles (Caretta Caretta); Zakynthos is one of the few places where the endangered Caretta Caretta turtles nest. These gentle creatures can be spotted in Laganas Bay and the National Marine Park, where conservation efforts help protect their habitat. Visitors can take eco-friendly boat tours to observe them up close.

Zakynthos Town; The island's capital is a charming blend of history and modern attractions. Stroll through its scenic streets, visit the Venetian Castle, admire the Church of St. Dionysios, and explore the Solomos Museum. Zakynthos Town also offers lively cafés, shopping, and waterfront dining.

without the peak-season crowds. This is also the time for vineyard harvests, making it an excellent season for wine lovers to explore local wineries. With fewer tourists and a more tranquil setting, autumn is perfect for a relaxed getaway.

Winter (November to March); Winter is the island's quietest season, with cooler temperatures ranging from 10°C to 15°C (50°F–59°F). Though not ideal for beach activities, it's a great time to experience Zakynthos' local culture, traditions, and historical sites without tourist crowds. The island remains beautiful, and visitors can explore markets, enjoy traditional cuisine, and take in the slower-paced lifestyle

Best Time to Visit; Spring and autumn provide pleasant weather, fewer crowds, and beautiful scenery, making them ideal for a laid-back trip. Summer is the best choice for those looking for beach fun and a vibrant atmosphere. Winter offers a peaceful experience, allowing visitors to immerse themselves in the island's authentic culture.

Visa And Tavelling Documents

Passport; Your passport should be valid for at least six months beyond your departure date from Greece. Ensure it has at least two blank pages for entry stamps.

Visa; Depending on your nationality, you may need a visa to enter Greece. A Schengen visa (Type C) allows stays of up to 90 days, while longer visits require a national visa (Type D).

Travel Insurance ; It's mandatory to have travel insurance covering emergency medical expenses, with a minimum coverage of €30,000.

Flight Tickets; Keep your round-trip flight tickets handy, as they are often required for visa applications and upon entry into Greece.

Proof of Accommodation; This could be a hotel reservation, a rental agreement, or a letter of invitation from a host in Greece.

Proof of Financial Means; Authorities may ask for evidence that you can support yourself during your stay, such as bank statements, pay slips, or a sponsorship letter.

Passenger Locator Form (PLF); Although not always mandateory, completing a PLF is recommended for contact tracing.

Packing List And Useful Apps

PASSPORT & TRAVEL DOCUMENTS; Ensure your passport is valid for at least six months beyond your planned departure date. Have all necessary travel documents, such as a visa (if required), insurance, and flight confirmations, neatly organized.

FLIGHT DETAILS; Carry a printed or digital copy of your flight itinerary for easy access when you arrive at the airport.

TRAVEL INSURANCE; It's crucial to have travel insurance that covers emergency medical expenses, lost baggage, or trip interruptions, giving you peace of mind during your stay.

MONEY & CARDS; While credit and debit cards are widely accepted, having some Euros on hand for small purchases like snacks or tips is a good idea.

PHONE & CHARGER; Your phone will be essential for navigation, staying connected, and using apps to help explore the island.

REUSABLE WATER BOTTLE ; Help stay hydrated while reducing plastic waste. You'll find plenty of spots to refill your bottle on the island, especially during hikes or beach visits.

SUNSCREEN & INSECT REPELLENT; Protect your skin from the sun's strong rays and prevent bug bites with a good sunscreen (SPF 30 or higher) and insect repellent.

HAT & SUNGLASSES ;A wide-brimmed hat and quality sunglasses are essential for comfort and protecting yourself from the sun.

COMFORTABLE SHOES ; A good pair of shoes is key for exploring the island's cobblestone streets, hiking trails, and beaches. Consider packing flip-flops for beach days and sturdy walking shoes for sightseeing.

SWIMWEAR; With the island's stunning beaches, you'll want to pack a couple of swimsuits for the days spent by the water.

LIGHT JACKET; While Zakynthos enjoys warm days, evenings can be cooler, especially by the sea, so a light jacket will come in handy.

DAYPACK; A small backpack or tote bag is great for carrying your essentials like water, sunscreen, and snacks while out on day trips.

BREATHABLE CLOTHING; Lightweight and breathable fabrics such as cotton or linen will keep you comfortable in Zakynthos' warm climate.

CAMERA; The island's natural beauty deserves to be captured. A good camera will help you preserve memories of Zakynthos' breathtaking landscapes and vibrant towns.

TRAVEL PILLOW & BLANKET ; If you're traveling by ferry to Zakynthos or have a long flight, having a travel pillow and blanket for extra comfort can make your journey much more pleasant.

Helpful Travel Apps

SKYSCANNER ; A top app for comparing flight prices and finding the best travel deals.

BOOKING.COM;Easily find and book accommodations, from budget options to luxury stays.

GOOGLE MAPS; Essential for getting around, finding attractions, and exploring Zakynthos with ease.

Currency And Banking

The official currency of Zakynthos, as with the rest of Greece, is the Euro (€). It's a good idea to exchange some money into Euros before your trip, as exchange rates are often better at home than at airports or in tourist areas. Credit and debit cards are accepted in most hotels, restaurants, and shops, but it's always helpful to carry some cash for smaller purchases and tips.

Banking in Zakynthos

- ✓ National Bank of Greece: Plateia Solomou 1, Zakynthos, 29100. Phone: +30 2695 021003.
- ✓ Alpha Bank: Plateia Agiou Markou, Zakynthos, 29100. Phone: +30 2695 042736.
- ✓ Eurobank: Leoforos Dimokratias 4, Zakynthos, 29100. Phone: +30 2695 026052.
- ✓ Piraeus Bank: Leoforos Venizelou 10, Ioannou Plessa, Zakynthos, 29100. Phone: +30 2695 306130.

ATMs are abundant, particularly in tourist zones, offering easy access to Euros. Be sure to inform your bank about your travel dates to prevent any issues with using your cards abroad.

Helpful Tips

Traditional Villages; For a taste of authentic Zakynthian life, visit villages like Keri, Volimes, and Maries. These charming spots feature stone-built houses, narrow alleys, and traditional tavernas serving homemade delicacies.

Beautiful Beaches; Beyond Navagio, Zakynthos boasts numerous stunning beaches. Gerakas is a nesting site for turtles, Banana Beach is perfect for sun-seekers, and Kalamaki offers a tranquil retreat.

Exciting Nightlife; The island offers a vibrant nightlife scene, especially in Laganas. With beach bars, clubs, and live music venues, visitors can dance the night away. For a more relaxed atmosphere, Zakynthos Town has elegant cocktail bars with stunning sea views.

Scenic Nature and Viewpoints; Zakynthos' beauty extends beyond its coastline. Rolling hills, olive groves, and panoramic spots like Bochali Hill provide breathtaking views

Diving and Snorkeling; The island's clear waters make it a paradise for underwater exploration. Dive sites like Keri Caves,

Marathonisi Island, and the Blue Caves are teeming with marine life, offering divers and snorkelers the chance to experience Zakynthos' underwater wonders.

Warm Hospitality; One of Zakynthos' greatest treasures is its people. The locals are known for their friendliness and hospitality, making visitors feel at home.

Dons And Donts

Dos:

Respect Nature: Zakynthos is home to protected areas like the National Marine Park. Always dispose of waste properly and avoid disturbing wildlife, especially the nesting sites of the Caretta Caretta turtles.

Embrace Local Traditions: The islanders are warm and welcoming, so return their kindness. A simple "Kalimera" (good morning) or "Kalispera" (good evening) goes a long way.

Savor Local Cuisine: Enjoy authentic Zakynthian flavors by dining at traditional tavernas. Be sure to try specialties like sartsa and ladotyri for a true taste of the island.

Dress Modestly at Religious Sites: While beach attire is perfect for the shore, covering shoulders and knees is expected when visiting churches and monasteries.

Join Local Celebrations: Zakynthos hosts vibrant cultural and religious festivals throughout the year. Participating in these events is a fantastic way to experience the island's traditions.

Don'ts:

Avoid Disturbing Wildlife: If you encounter the endangered loggerhead turtles, observe from a respectful distance and never attempt to touch or feed them.

Do Not Litter: Help preserve the island's beauty by using designated trash bins. Littering harms both the environment and the stunning scenery.

Follow Local Rules: Be aware of beach and marine park regulations to ensure a smooth and enjoyable stay.

Keep Noise Levels in Check: While Zakynthos has a lively nightlife, respect residential areas by keeping noise to a minimum.

ESSENTIAL PLANNING

Best Time To Visit

Spring (April to June); Spring is a wonderful time to explore Zakynthos. The weather is comfortably warm, with temperatures between 15°C and 25°C (59°F–77°F). The island bursts into color with wildflowers and lush greenery, creating a stunning landscape. This season is perfect for hiking, sightseeing, and enjoying nature without the summer crowds.

Summer (July to August); Summer is the height of the tourist season, with temperatures soaring between 25°C and 35°C (77°F–95°F). It's the best time for beach lovers, as the warm sea is ideal for swimming, snorkeling, and diving. Popular spots like Navagio Beach and Laganas Beach are lively, with plenty of activities and nightlife.

Autumn (September to October; Autumn offers warm temperatures ranging from 20°C to 30°C (68°F–86°F) and a calmer atmosphere. The sea remains inviting for swimming, and September, in particular, provides a summer-like experience

Exchange Rates: Always check the latest exchange rates before departing, so you have an idea of how much you'll need in cash.

Cash vs. Card: While credit and debit cards are widely accepted, some smaller shops and local markets might prefer cash.

Safety: Keep your cash and cards safe, and be cautious when withdrawing from ATMs, especially after dark.

SIM Cards And Internet

Germanos: A reliable option in Zakynthos town, Germanos offers SIM cards that can be easily activated with your passport for identification.

Local Phone Shops: You'll find numerous phone shops throughout Zakynthos town, all offering SIM cards for both short- and long-term use.

Athens Airport: While Zakynthos Airport doesn't have SIM card shops, you can purchase one at Athens Airport before heading to the island, ensuring you're connected as soon as you land.

Internet Access in Zakynthos

ZanteNetWiFi: This local provider offers wireless internet with speeds up to 40 Mbps, ensuring good coverage even in more remote areas of the island. They offer affordable packages starting at €20 per month, perfect for those who need reliable internet during their stay.

Free Wi-Fi: Many hotels, cafes, and restaurants around Zakynthos provide free Wi-Fi for their customers, making it easy to stay connected while you explore or relax.

Mini phrases to know

- Kalimera (καλημέρα) - Good morning.
- Kalispera (καλησπέρα) - Good evening.
- Kalinichta (καληνύχτα) - Good night.
- Geia sou (γεια σου) - Hello/Hi (informal).
- Geia sas (γεια σας) - Hello/Hi (formal).
- Ti kaneis? (Τι κάνεις;) - How are you? (informal).
- Ti kanete? (Τι κάνετε;) - How are you? (formal).
- Efcharistó (ευχαριστώ) - Thank you.
- Parakaló (παρακαλώ) - Please/You're welcome.
- Sygnómi (συγγνώμη) - Sorry/Excuse me.
- Ne (ναι) - Yes.

- Ochi (όχι) - No.
- Endáxei (εντάξει) - Okay.
- Póso kostízei? (Πόσο κοστίζει;) - How much does it cost?
- Pou ine…? (Που είναι…;) - Where is…?
- To logariasmó, parakaló (Το λογαριασμό, παρακαλώ) - The bill, please.
- Boró na écho…? (Μπορώ να έχω…;) - Can I have…?
- Neró (νερό) - Water.
- Kafé (καφέ) - Coffee.
- Psomí (ψωμί) - Bread.
- Eláte (ελάτε) - Come here.
- Epísi (επίσης) - You too/Also.
- Kalós írthate (Καλώς ήρθατε) - Welcome.
- Kalí órexi (Καλή όρεξη) - Enjoy your meal.
- Polí oreo (Πολύ ωραίο) - Very good/beautiful.
- Ti ora einai? (Τι ώρα είναι;) - What time is it?
- Echete pliroseis? (Έχετε πληρωμές;) - Do you accept payments?
- Théo na to doskido (Θέλω να το δοκιμάσω) - I want to try it.
- Anichto (ανοιχτό) - Open.

- Zante Emergency Health Care: Laganas, Machairado, Ionian Islands, 29092

Police and Fire Services:

- Zakynthos Police Department: +30 2695 022100
- Laganas Police Department: +30 2695 051251 or +30 2695 052022
- Fire Department: +30 2695 022161

Other Useful Contacts:

- Tourist Police Office: +30 2695 023467
- Port Authority: +30 2695 028117
- Bus Station (KTEL): +30 2695 022255 or +30 2695 042656
- Pharmacies: There are several pharmacies in Zakynthos, including Paraski Marietta, Mouzakis Tzanetos, and Hartas Angelos

Additional Resources:

- Zakynthos Port Authority: +30 2695 028117
- Levante Ferries: +30 2109 499400
- Zakynthos Airport: +30 2695 029500

➢ Taxi Services: Zante Taxi (+30 2695 77573020), Spiros Taxi (+30 2695 78100704), TaxiCabZante (+30 2695 033300)

Local Etiquette In Zakynthos

Greetings: Zakynthians are known for their warm hospitality and friendly nature. It's customary to greet people with a "Kalimera" (good morning) or "Kalispera" (good evening), depending on the time of day. If you're meeting someone for the first time, "Geia sou" (hello) is a polite and casual greeting, while "Geia sas" is used when addressing a group or someone in a more formal context.

Dress Modestly: While casual beachwear is acceptable along the coast, it's important to dress modestly when visiting churches and monasteries. Cover your shoulders and knees as a sign of respect, particularly in places of worship or more conservative areas. This shows consideration for local customs and traditions.

Table Manners: Dining is an important part of Greek culture, and sharing meals is a sign of hospitality. When dining out, it's polite to wait for the host to invite you to sit. Greeks often share food, so don't be surprised if you're offered various dishes to try.

Complimenting the food with a "Poli oreo!" (very good!) and saying "Efcharistó" (thank you) will surely be appreciated by your hosts.

Respect for Religious Sites: Zakynthos is home to several churches and monasteries that are integral to the local culture. When visiting these religious sites, always maintain a respectful tone. It's important to avoid loud conversations, keep your phone off, and refrain from taking photographs unless you're given explicit permission. This ensures that you're respecting the sacred nature of these locations.

Tipping: Tipping is a common practice in Greece, especially in restaurants and cafes. A tip of 5-10% is generally appreciated for good service. It's also customary to leave a small tip for taxi drivers, hotel staff, and tour guides, as a token of appreciation for their help and service.

Personal Space: Greeks are known for their friendly and open nature, often engaging in close physical contact when conversing. However, it's important to be mindful of personal space, especially if you're unfamiliar with the culture.

TRANSPORTATION OPTIONS

Getting There

By Plane:

Direct Flights: Zakynthos International Airport (ZTH) welcomes direct flights from Athens and a number of European cities, particularly in the summer months (May to October). Airlines such as Aegean, Olympic Air, Sky Express, Ryanair, Volotea, Wizzair, and EasyJet operate these routes.

Flight Duration: The flight from Athens to Zakynthos takes approximately 50 minutes.

Airport Location: The airport is just 3 km away from Zakynthos town, making it easily accessible by car, bus, or taxi.

By Ferry:

From the Mainland: Ferries leave daily from the port of Killini on the western Peloponnese to Zakynthos Port, with a journey time of about 75 minutes.

From Kefalonia: There are ferry connections between Zakynthos and Kefalonia, with a crossing time of around 1.5 hours.

From Italy: During the summer (July and August), ferries run between Zakynthos Port and the Italian cities of Bari and Brindisi. The crossing takes approximately 17 hours.

By Bus:

From Athens: You can catch a bus from Athens to Zakynthos, which includes a ferry ride from Killini. The total journey time is roughly 6 hours.

From Patra: Another bus option is from Patra to Zakynthos, which also involves a ferry ride from Killini. This trip takes around 3 hours.

Local Transportation:

Car Rentals: Renting a car is an ideal way to explore Zakynthos independently. There are multiple car rental services available on the island.

Taxis: Taxis are readily available and provide a convenient way to get around, especially for those who prefer not to drive.

Ferry Options

From the Mainland:

Killini to Zakynthos: Ferries operate daily from the port of Killini, located on the western Peloponnese, to Zakynthos Port. This scenic journey takes approximately 75 minutes, offering travelers a pleasant trip across the Ionian Sea.

Ferry Companies: Levante Ferries, Ionian Ferries.

Departure Times: Multiple departures throughout the day, including early morning, mid-day, and late evening. During the high tourist season, ferries are more frequent to accommodate the increase in visitors.

Frequency: High frequency during the peak months of May to October. It's advisable to check ferry schedules in advance during busy times, as they can fill up quickly.

Onboard Facilities: Some ferries offer amenities such as cafes, lounges, and outdoor seating areas, making the ride comfortable. Passengers can enjoy views of the coastline and nearby islands as they travel.

Patra to Zakynthos: Ferries also operate from the port of Patra to Zakynthos, with a brief stop at Killini. This option allows travelers to continue their journey from Patra without needing to switch ferries at Killini. The total travel time is about 3 hours.

Departure Times: Ferries from Patra typically depart a few times a day. Similar to the Killini to Zakynthos route, it's important to check schedules ahead of time.

Frequency: These ferries are available year-round, with increased frequency during peak travel seasons.

From Kefalonia:

Kefalonia to Zakynthos: There are regular ferry routes between Zakynthos and Kefalonia, with a crossing time of approximately 1.5 hours. This route is ideal for travelers looking to combine visits to both islands, as they are located close to each other in the Ionian Sea.

Ferry Companies: Ionian Ferries.

Departure Times: Departures occur several times throughout the day, making it easy to plan your trip.

Frequency: Ferries run frequently during the tourist season, especially in the summer months, providing flexibility for travelers.

From Italy:

Bari to Zakynthos: During the summer months (July and August), ferries operate between the Italian ports of Bari and Zakynthos Port. The journey takes about 17 hours, with overnight ferries allowing passengers to sleep on board.

Ferry Companies: Various operators, including Levante Ferries.

Departure Times: Most ferries depart in the evening, so travelers can enjoy a peaceful night crossing and arrive in Zakynthos by morning.

Frequency: This route operates primarily during the summer months, with ferries departing a few times each week.

Onboard Experience: These ferries are typically equipped with cabins, dining areas, and lounges for passengers to relax during the journey. Booking a cabin is recommended for added comfort, especially for those traveling overnight.

Tips for Ferry Travel:

Booking Tickets: During the high season, it's advisable to book ferry tickets in advance, especially for popular routes like Killini to Zakynthos. You can often book tickets online or through travel agents on the island.

Arriving Early: Arrive at the ferry terminal at least 30 minutes before departure, particularly during busy periods. This allows time for parking, check-in, and boarding.

Luggage: Most ferries have designated areas for luggage. Larger items like bikes or extra baggage may incur additional fees, so be sure to check with the ferry company before your trip.

Public Transport

KTEL Buses

Zakynthos Town to Tsilivi & Tragaki: Frequent service throughout the day on weekdays and Saturdays, with three routes on Sundays.

Zakynthos Town to Alykes & Ammousi: Five daily routes on weekdays and Saturdays, no service on Sundays.

Zakynthos Town to Argassi: Multiple daily services on weekdays and Saturdays, with two routes on Sundays.

Zakynthos Town to Vasilikos - Banana - Agios Nikolaos Beach - Porto Roma: Six routes daily on weekdays and Saturdays, two on Sundays.

Zakynthos Town to Laganas: Multiple services throughout the day on weekdays and Saturdays, with five routes on Sundays.

Zakynthos Town to Kalamaki: Frequent routes on weekdays and Saturdays, five routes on Sundays.

Zakynthos Town to Zakynthos Airport: Six routes daily.

Ticket Price: €1.80 per journey.

Taxis

Zante Taxi: +30 2695 77573020

Spiros Taxi: +30 2695 78100704

TaxiCabZante: +30 2695 033300

Car Rentals

Water Taxis

Taxi4u.com: This service specializes in both land and water taxi transfers. They provide online booking, ensuring ease and flexibility for travelers heading to and from the port or airport.

Stathmos Taxi: Known for their commitment to safety and customer service, Stathmos Taxi offers water taxi services to various popular spots around the island.

ZanteLimo: If you're looking for a more luxurious way to travel, ZanteLimo offers premium private transfers, including water taxis. Their fleet of luxury vehicles ensures a stylish and comfortable ride.

Island Hopping Tours

Zakynthos: One Day Small Group Tour to Navagio Beach, Blue Caves & Top View: A fantastic full-day tour that allows you to visit Zakynthos' most famous sights, including the iconic Navagio Beach and the Blue Caves, while enjoying stunning panoramic views of the island.

Excursion to Olympia Archaeological Site from Zakynthos: This two-day excursion offers a unique opportunity to explore the ancient birthplace of the Olympic Games. A ferry ride to the mainland adds to the adventure, followed by a visit to Olympia's UNESCO-listed archaeological site.

Laganas Zakynthos: Marathonissi, Keri Caves and Turtles Spotting: This half-day tour is perfect for nature enthusiasts and families. Departing from Laganas Beach, you'll have the chance to spot loggerhead sea turtles and explore the picturesque Keri Caves.

Private 7m 250hp Speed Boat Tour Shipwreck Blue Caves up to 8 Pax: For those looking for an exclusive and personalized experience, this premium tour takes you on a private boat to visit Shipwreck Beach and the Blue Caves. With a small group of up to 8 people, you can enjoy these incredible sites in privacy and style.

Tips For Renting A Car In Zakynthos

Book Ahead for the Best Deals: Especially in the busy tourist season (May to October), it's advisable to reserve your car rental in advance.

Check for Extra Fees: Make sure to review the rental agreement carefully for hidden charges such as insurance costs, fuel fees, or penalties for late returns. Don't hesitate to ask the rental company about any unclear terms.

Choose the Right Vehicle: Think about the kind of terrain you'll be driving on. If you plan to explore the island's more rugged areas, an SUV with higher ground clearance is a smart choice. For lighter, more casual driving, a compact car may suffice.

Inspect the Car: Before hitting the road, thoroughly check the car for any pre-existing damages and ensure these are noted on your rental agreement. This avoids disputes when you return the vehicle.

Familiarize Yourself with Local Driving Rules: To ensure a safe trip, familiarize yourself with Zakynthos' driving laws, such as speed limits and parking regulations. Understanding local road rules can help prevent fines and accidents.

Be Prepared for Navigation and Parking: Whether you opt for a car with GPS or use your smartphone for navigation, make sure you have a reliable way to find your way around. Also, be mindful that parking in popular tourist areas and Zakynthos Town can be tricky, so always look for designated spots and avoid parking in restricted zones.

ACCOMMODATION

Luxury Hotels And Resorts

Lesante Cape Resort & Villas

- Address: Akrotiri, Zakynthos, 29092, Greece

This 5-star resort offers an exclusive stay with luxurious villas that come with private pools, creating a serene environment for relaxation. The resort features a seasonal outdoor swimming pool, a modern fitness center, and a private beach for guests to enjoy

Lesante Blu, a member of The Leading Hotels of the World

- Address: Tragaki, Zakynthos, 29092, Greece

A luxurious beach resort offering the perfect blend of modern comfort and exclusive amenities. It features stunning infinity pools, a comprehensive spa center, and three diverse restaurants serving a range of cuisines including Greek and Mediterranean options, as well as an American breakfast.

Votsalon Beach House : Alykes Beach, Zakynthos, 29090, Right on Alykes Beach, this beach house provides a relaxed atmosphere with direct access to the sand and sea. It's a great choice for those looking to enjoy the beach without spending too much.

Artemis Apartments : Meso Gerakari, Kipseli, 29100, Just a short distance from Gerakari Beach, Artemis Apartments features a sun-drenched terrace with loungers and a small playground. This place is perfect for families and beach lovers who want to relax in a peaceful setting.

Zakynthos Hostel : Zakynthos Town, Zakynthos, 29092, Located in Zakynthos Town, this budget-friendly hostel offers dormitory-style rooms and a communal vibe, making it an ideal spot for solo travelers and backpackers looking to meet new people.

Family -Friendly Stays And Hostels

Letsos Hotel: Just a short walk from Alykanas Beach, Letsos Hotel offers spacious guestrooms with private balconies or patios, making it a great choice for families seeking comfortable accommodations with convenient beach access, Alykanas, Alykes, 29090

Phoenix Hotel Zakynthos: Located near the historical Dionysios Solomos square, Phoenix Hotel Zakynthos provides modernly decorated rooms with stunning views over the port and the Ionian Sea. It's an ideal spot for families visiting Zakynthos for both leisure and work, Solomos Square 2, Zakynthos Town, 29100

San Salvatore : Agios Sostis, Zakynthos Town, 29092, Situated right on the beach, San Salvatore offers families beachfront accommodations with free Wi-Fi and on-site parking. It's a peaceful choice for those who want to enjoy a relaxing stay close to the water.

Elea Hotel Apartments and Villas : Argasion, Argasi, 29100, This family-friendly hotel offers apartments and villas equipped with kitchenettes, refrigerators, and air conditioning. Guests can enjoy the pool and free Wi-Fi, making it a popular option for families visiting the Argassi area.

Choosing The Right Accomodations

Luxury Resorts

Lesante Cape Resort & Villas – Akrotiri, Zakynthos, 29092

Lesante Blu, a member of The Leading Hotels of the World – Tragaki, Zakynthos, 29092

Porto Zante Villas & Spa – Tsilivi, Zakynthos, 29092

Olea All Suite Hotel – Tsilivi, Zakynthos, 29092

Cielo Villas Hotel – Zakynthos Town, Zakynthos, 29092

Family-Friendly Stays

Letsos Hotel – Alykanas, Alykes, 29090

Phoenix Hotel Zakynthos – Solomos Square 2, Zakynthos Town, 29100

San Salvatore – Agios Sostis, Zakynthos Town, 29092

Elea Hotel Apartments and Villas – Argasion, Argasi, 29100

Budget-Friendly Hostels and Guesthouses

Anatoli Labreon – Agia Marina, Zakynthos, 29100

Pine Tree Apartment Sunset – 12 KOILIOMENO, Koiliomenos, Ionian Islands, 29092

Artemis Apartments – Meso Gerakari, Kipseli, 29100

Zakynthos Hostel – Zakynthos Town, Zakynthos, 29092

Key Considerations When Choosing Accommodation:

Location: Think about the attractions and activities you plan to explore. Zakynthos Town is perfect for those who want easy access to restaurants, shops, and nightlife, while quieter areas like Vasilikos are ideal for a peaceful retreat.

Amenities: List the essential amenities, such as Wi-Fi, pools, beach access, or family-friendly features. This will help you find accommodations that meet your needs.

Reviews: Check traveler reviews on websites like Tripadvisor, Booking.com, or Google to gain insight into the quality and service of the accommodation.

Budget: Establish a budget for your trip and find places within your range. Don't forget to include additional costs such as food, transportation, and activities.

explore the caves by boat, and those wanting to experience the water up close can enjoy snorkeling in the crystal-clear depths.

Porto Vromi

- Address: Near Navagio Beach, Zakynthos, 29092, Greece
- Opening Hours: Accessible 24/7
- Activities: Beach lounging, swimming
- Entry Fee: Free

Porto Vromi is a small, secluded beach offering a peaceful escape from the crowds. With its calm waters and charming setting, it's an ideal spot to unwind, swim, and relax. The beach's white pebbles and crystal-clear waters create an idyllic environment for a quieter day by the sea.

Anafonitria Monastery

- Address: Near Navagio Beach, Zakynthos, 29092, Greece
- Opening Hours: 8:00 AM - 5:00 PM (Monastery), 24/7 (Monastery grounds)
- Activities: Historical exploration, photography

- ❖ Entry Fee: Free

The Anafonitria Monastery, founded in the 16th century, offers a glimpse into the spiritual and historical heritage of Zakynthos. Set against a backdrop of lush greenery, the monastery is an important religious site and provides a serene escape from the beach.

Xigia Beach

- ❖ Address: Near Navagio Beach, Zakynthos, 29092, Greece
- ❖ Opening Hours: Accessible 24/7
- ❖ Activities: Snorkeling, swimming
- ❖ Entry Fee: Free

Xigia Beach is famous for its natural hot springs, which flow into the sea, giving the water a unique, therapeutic quality. The warm mineral-rich waters create a rejuvenating experience for swimmers and snorkelers. It's a peaceful and scenic spot, perfect for those looking to enjoy both relaxation and natural healing in a beautiful setting.

Blue Caves

Blue Caves Overview

Location: Situated along the northwest coast of Zakynthos, between the port of Agios Nikolaos and Cape Skinari.

Activities: Boat tours, snorkeling, kayaking.

Entry Fee: Varies by tour operator.

Opening Hours: The caves are accessible 24/7, though boat tours operate within set times.

How to Visit

1. By Boat: The most popular way to explore the Blue Caves is by boat. Tours typically depart from Zakynthos Town harbor or Agios Nikolaos port and often include visits to other landmarks like Navagio Beach.

2. By Private Boat: For a more personalized experience, you can rent a private boat, either with a captain or on your own. This option offers the freedom to explore the caves at your own pace.

3. By Kayak: For the more adventurous traveler, kayaking to the Blue Caves is an option. Be sure to check sea conditions and adhere to safety guidelines before setting out.

What to Expect

Natural Beauty: The Blue Caves are famous for their strikingly blue waters, which shimmer as they reflect off the cave walls, creating a truly magical atmosphere.

Rock Formations: The caves boast fascinating rock formations, including arches and tunnels, shaped by years of natural erosion.

Wildlife: The surrounding waters are rich in marine life, making it a fantastic spot for snorkeling and observing the underwater world.

Tips for Visiting

Weather Conditions: Always check the weather and sea conditions before planning your visit, as boat tours may be canceled if the seas are too rough.

you're hiking along the cliffside or simply soaking in the scenery, this location is perfect for nature lovers and photographers alike. It's also a great place to relax and enjoy a refreshing drink at the viewpoint station while watching the sunset or the boats passing by. The cliffs are a peaceful spot, ideal for those looking to escape the crowds and appreciate the island's natural beauty.

Keri Lighthouse

Location: Keri Village, Zakynthos, 290 90, Greece, 10:00 AM - 10:00 PM

Activities: Dining, sightseeing, photography, Free (dining fees apply)

The Keri Lighthouse, perched atop the cliffs, offers breathtaking views of the sea, and is a peaceful retreat for visitors seeking tranquility. The surrounding area is home to a cozy cliffside restaurant where you can indulge in delicious meals, including vegetarian options, all while watching the sun set over the horizon. It's an ideal spot for an evening dinner or a casual drink as you take in the beauty of the surrounding landscape.

Keri Caves

Location: Off the coast of Keri Village, Accessible 24/7 (via boat tours)

Activities: Boat tours, swimming, snorkeling, Entry Fee: Varies by tour operator

The Keri Caves are an impressive network of sea caves located on the coast of Keri. These caves can only be accessed by boat, and the deep blue waters and stunning limestone formations create a mesmerizing setting. It's a great place for adventurous visitors to explore by boat or kayak, or simply swim in the cool, clear waters.

Marathonisi (Turtle Island)

Marathonisi (Turtle Island) : Laganas Bay, Zakynthos, 290 90, Greece, Accessible 24/7, Turtle spotting, swimming, snorkeling, sightseeing, Free (boat tour fees apply), Marathonisi is a picturesque islet in Laganas Bay, serving as a vital breeding ground for loggerhead sea turtles. Visitors can take boat tours to spot these magnificent creatures in their natural habitat.

Marathonisi Beaches : Marathonisi Island, Zakynthos, 290 90, Greece, Accessible 24/7, Swimming, sunbathing, snorkeling, Free, The beaches of Marathonisi Island are famous for their crystal-clear waters and idyllic setting. The northern beach, a turtle nesting area, is largely off-limits to protect the wildlife, while the southern beach offers a tranquil spot for swimming and sunbathing.

Sea Caves : Marathonisi Island, Zakynthos, 290 90, Greece, Accessible 24/7, Swimming, snorkeling, exploring, Free, The sea caves on Marathonisi Island are one of the island's most popular attractions. These caves provide an unforgettable underwater experience, with clear waters and stunning rock formations, ideal for swimming and snorkeling.

Boat Tours : Depart from Laganas Bay, Zakynthos, 290 90, Greece, *Opening Hours:* Vary by operator, typically from early morning to late afternoon, Guided boat tours, turtle spotting, snorkeling , *Entry Fee*: Varies by tour operator. Boat tours to Marathonisi Island allow visitors to explore the island and its surroundings.

Scenic Views : Marathonisi Island, Zakynthos, 290 90, Greece, Accessible 24/7, Sightseeing, photography, Free. Marathonisi Island offers stunning panoramic views of the Ionian Sea and the nearby landscape. Its natural beauty makes it a perfect destination for sightseeing and photography, especially during the golden hours of sunrise and sunset.

Wildlife Conservation : Marathonisi Island, Zakynthos, 290 90, Greece, Accessible 24/7, Learning about wildlife conservation, turtle spotting, Free. As a key site for the conservation of loggerhead sea turtles, Marathonisi Island plays an important role in protecting these endangered creatures. Visitors can learn about ongoing conservation efforts and observe turtles in their natural environment.

Bohali Hill

BOCHALI VIEWPOINT: The Bochali Viewpoint offers spectacular panoramic views over Zakynthos Town and the Ionian Sea. It's a favorite location for visitors seeking to capture the beauty of the island and snap some breathtaking photos of the landscape. Bochali Hill, Zakynthos, 290 90, Greece of Saint Nikolaos, the Byzantine Museum, and the Cultural Centre of Zakynthos. It's a popular gathering spot for both locals and tourists, providing a peaceful atmosphere and beautiful surroundings.

Zakynthos Town

Zakynthos, 29100, Greece, Accessible 24/7, Free, As the island's capital, Zakynthos Town offers a delightful blend of history and modern life. Strolling through its narrow streets, visitors can explore charming local shops, dine at traditional tavernas, and admire the town's distinctive architecture. It's an energetic town with a vibrant atmosphere, perfect for spending a leisurely day.

Church of Saint Nikolaos

Zakynthos Town, Zakynthos, 29100, Greece, 09:00 AM - 05:00 PM, Free, Dating back to 1561, the Church of Saint Nikolaos is one of the oldest in Zakynthos Town. It withstood the devastating 1953 earthquake and remains an important historical and architectural landmark. Visitors can admire its beauty and learn about its significance in the town's rich history.

Byzantine Museum

Zakynthos Town, Zakynthos, 29100, Greece, 09:00 AM - 05:00 PM, Free, The Byzantine Museum in Zakynthos Town displays a fascinating collection of artifacts from the island's Byzantine era. It offers an opportunity to delve into the island's history and view interesting exhibitions that highlight its cultural evolution.

Cultural Centre of Zakynthos

Zakynthos Town, Zakynthos, 29100, Greece, 09:00 AM - 05:00 PM, Free, The Cultural Centre of Zakynthos is home to a library, art gallery, and various exhibitions. It serves as a hub for cultural events, making it an ideal spot for visitors to learn about local traditions and immerse themselves in the island's artistic heritage.

Local Shops and Cafés

Zakynthos Town, Zakynthos, 29100, Greece, Free. Zakynthos Town offers a variety of local shops and cafés where visitors can purchase unique souvenirs, savor local dishes, and unwind. The lively town atmosphere, combined with its friendly locals, creates an inviting environment for exploration.

Zakynthos' Villages

Zakynthos Town (Chora)

Zakynthos Town, or Chora, is the island's capital, offering a blend of historical charm and modern amenities. Visitors can wander through its narrow streets, browse local shops, and enjoy traditional dining. The town is known for its lively atmosphere and captivating architecture, making it a great place to explore. Zakynthos, 29100, Greece, Accessible 24/7, Free

Argassi

Argassi is a popular resort located near Zakynthos Town and the airport. It features a beautiful beach, a range of water sports, and a vibrant nightlife scene with bars, clubs, and restaurants. It's an ideal spot for both relaxation and fun. Zakynthos, 29100, Greece, Accessible 24/7, Free

Volimes

Volimes is a charming agricultural village situated on the island's northern side. It offers breathtaking views of the surrounding landscape and provides a tranquil, rural atmosphere for those seeking peace and natural beauty. Zakynthos, 29100, Greece, Accessible 24/7, Free

Maries: Maries is a peaceful village offering stunning views of the Ionian Sea. Untouched by mass tourism, it provides an authentic glimpse into the traditional rural life of Zakynthos. Zakynthos, 29100, Greece, Accessible 24/7, Free

Agios Leon; Agios Leon is a quaint village located on the western side of Zakynthos. Named after a 14th-century church, it boasts a charming, historical ambiance that makes it perfect for those interested in the island's heritage. Zakynthos, 29100, Greece, Accessible 24/7, Free

ZAKYNTHIAN CUISINE

Traditional Cuisine

Kolokithokeftedes (Zucchini Balls) : Zakynthos Island, Greece, Kolokithokeftedes are crispy, golden-brown fritters made from a combination of grated zucchini, feta cheese, onions, and fresh mint. These savory balls are typically served as an appetizer or side dish and are often paired with a refreshing yogurt dip or tzatziki for added flavor.

Tzatziki : Zakynthos Island, Greece, Tzatziki is a classic Greek dip made from thick, creamy yogurt, crisp cucumbers, garlic, dill, and a touch of extra virgin olive oil. This refreshing, tangy dip is a staple in Greek cuisine, enjoyed with pita bread, grilled meats, or as a side dish

Greek Salad (Horiatiki) : Zakynthos Island, Greece, The Greek salad, or Horiatiki, is a refreshing and vibrant dish, perfect for the warm Mediterranean climate. It's made with juicy tomatoes, crunchy cucumbers, red onions, green peppers, black olives, and generous chunks of feta cheese, all drizzled with high-quality olive oil and sprinkled with oregano

Moussaka : Zakynthos Island, Greece, Moussaka is a rich, comforting Greek dish that layers eggplant, potatoes, and minced meat cooked in a savory tomato sauce.

Halloumi Cheese : Zakynthos Island, Greece, Halloumi is a semi-hard, unripened cheese made from goat's milk, which is often grilled or fried due to its high melting point. With a firm, slightly salty taste, it pairs wonderfully with fresh salads, vegetables, or even on its own as a snack.

Gyros : Zakynthos Island, Greece, Gyros is perhaps the most famous of Greek street foods, and Zakynthos does it exceptionally well. It consists of meat, typically pork or chicken, cooked on a vertical rotisserie until crispy on the outside, tender on the inside

Must-Try Dishes And Street Food

Bourdeto : Available at various tavernas in Zakynthos Town

Bourdeto is a bold, spicy fish stew typically made with scorpion fish or other firm white fish. The dish is simmered in a rich, flavorful broth made from tomatoes, onions, and a generous amount of hot paprika, delivering a deliciously spicy kick.

Saganaki : Found at various street food stalls in Zakynthos Town, Saganaki is a tasty fried cheese appetizer, typically made from kefalotyri or graviera cheese.

Pastitsio : Served in numerous tavernas in Zakynthos Town, Pastitsio is a comforting baked pasta dish, similar to lasagna, that layers pasta with seasoned ground meat (usually beef or lamb) and a rich béchamel sauce.

Stifado : Found in various tavernas around Zakynthos Town, Stifado is a slow-cooked stew typically made with beef or rabbit, onions, tomatoes, and a fragrant blend of spices like cinnamon and cloves.

Kleftiko : Available at different tavernas in Zakynthos Town, Kleftiko is a traditional Greek dish where lamb is marinated in garlic, lemon, and herbs, then slow-cooked in a sealed parcel, allowing the meat to retain all its juicy flavor. The result is tender, flavorful meat that falls off the bone.

Fasolada : Served in tavernas across Zakynthos Town, Fasolada is a traditional Greek bean soup made with white beans, tomatoes, carrots, celery, and olive oil. It's a hearty, nourishing dish and is often regarded as Greece's national dish due to its simple, wholesome ingredients.

Top Restaurants, Cafés, And Dining Spots

Fiore Fine Dining: Offering stunning views and a refined dining experience, Fiore blends European and Greek flavors, emphasizing fresh, premium ingredients in every dish. Zakynthos Town

The Halfway House: This upscale restaurant serves both international and Mediterranean cuisine. It's an ideal spot for a memorable meal, complete with breathtaking views. Tsilivi

Zorbas Greek Taverna: Renowned for its delicious chicken souvlaki and gyros, Zorbas Greek Taverna is a must-try for anyone craving authentic Greek cuisine paired with excellent service. Zakynthos Town

Restaurant Keri Lighthouse: Situated near the iconic lighthouse, this restaurant specializes in fresh seafood and Mediterranean dishes, all served with stunning sea views. Keri

Palatium: Palatium offers a mix of Italian and American dishes, from fillet steak to pasta, all served in a cozy, welcoming atmosphere. Zakynthos Town

Green Frog: Popular for its Mediterranean offerings, Green Frog combines great food with a relaxed ambiance, making it a favorite spot for both locals and visitors. Zakynthos Town

Zakynthian Wines And Vineyards

Ktima Grampsa : Stravopodi 16, Zakynthos, Greece, Nestled in a picturesque location, Ktima Grampsa is renowned for its exceptional wines made from locally grown grape varieties.

Goumas Estate - Art & Wine Winery : Zakynthos, Greece**,** At Goumas Estate, wine lovers can indulge in a unique blend of art and wine. This winery offers a memorable experience where visitors can savor freshly baked bread, local olive oil, cheese, and figs, perfectly paired with their range of exquisite wines.

Solomos Wines : Zakynthos, Greece, Solomos Wines is a place where tradition meets flavor. The winery is celebrated for its selection of wines that beautifully capture the essence of Zakynthos' rich heritage, making it a must-visit for anyone seeking to explore the island's local wines.

Ampelostrates Horse Vineyard : Zakynthos, Greece. Situated in the heart of a sprawling vineyard, Ampelostrates Horse Vineyard combines wine tasting with a true taste of Zakynthian life.

Oenolpi Winery : Zakynthos, Greece, Oenolpi Winery offers an engaging wine tour and tasting experience, guided by knowledgeable staff who share their expertise on the island's unique winemaking traditions.

Local Crafts And Handicrafts

Gabrielis Art Works : Georgiou Moothonaiou, opposite KTEZ Zakynthos, Zakynthos, 291 00, Greece, Gabrielis Art Works is renowned for its stunning handmade pottery and ceramics, offering a wide array of distinctive and artistic pieces that reflect the craftsmanship of Zakynthian artisans.

films. Many screenings take place in picturesque outdoor settings, making it a unique cultural experience under the stars. Various locations in Zakynthos, including outdoor venues

Zakynthos Art Festival: An annual celebration of creativity, the Zakynthos Art Festival features a diverse mix of visual arts, theater, dance, and music. Zakynthos Town, Greece

Panayiria: A traditional countryside festival, Panayiria takes place in the island's rural villages and includes religious processions, fairs, and community gatherings. Rural villages of Zakynthos, Greece

Churches And Monasteries

CHURCH OF SAINT DIONYSIOS : Zakynthos Town, near the port, Dedicated to the island's patron saint, the Church of Saint Dionysios is a significant religious site featuring a towering bell tower, the tallest in Zakynthos

MONASTERY OF PANAGIA SKOPIOTISSA : Argassi Village, Perched on a hill above Argassi, this monastery offers stunning views of the island. Though partly in ruins, its historical significance and the tranquil natural setting make it a worthwhile visit for those seeking a peaceful escape.

MONASTERY OF PANAGIA ANAFONITRIA : Plemonari, Zakynthos. Nestled in a serene pine forest, the Monastery of Panagia Anafonitria is a popular pilgrimage site. Visitors can admire a 15th-century icon of the Virgin Mary and explore the monastery's exquisite wall frescoes, making it a must-visit for those interested in religious art and history.

Tops Museums

<u>Byzantine Museum of Zakynthos</u> : Plateia Dionysiou Solomou, Zakynthos, Ionian Islands, 29100. The Byzantine Museum showcases an impressive collection of 17th-century icons and religious artifacts, many of which were saved from destruction during the 1953 earthquake

<u>Aristeon Olive Press & Museum</u> : Lithakia, Zante, 290 92, This fascinating museum offers an in-depth look into the island's olive oil production history. Visitors can explore traditional olive presses and learn about the modern, sustainable methods used today to produce olive oil.

<u>Museum of D. Solomos and Eminent People of Zakynthos</u> : Agios Markos Square, Zakynthos Town. Dedicated to the famous poet Dionysios Solomos and other prominent figures from Zakynthos, this museum features personal belongings, manuscripts, and artwork that highlight the island's cultural heritage.

<u>Helmi's Natural History Museum</u> : Agia Marina, Zakynthos. Helmi's Museum provides an educational experience focusing on Zakynthos' diverse flora, fauna, and marine life. With over 1,500 specimens, it's a great place for visitors of all ages to learn about the island's natural environment.

Historical And Cultural Landmarks

Venetian Castle of Zakynthos

Bochali, Zakynthos Town. Perched above Zakynthos Town, this historic castle provides stunning panoramic views of the town and its surroundings. It's an ideal spot for visitors to explore the island's Venetian heritage while taking in the scenic beauty.

Kampi Cross

Kampi, Zakynthos. This prominent cement cross stands as a memorial to those who lost their lives during the civil war. Visible from a distance, it serves as a poignant reminder of the island's turbulent past.

Solomos and Kalvos Museum

Saint Mark's Square, Zakynthos Town. This museum honors the renowned poets Dionysios Solomos and Andreas Kalvos. It displays personal belongings, manuscripts, and various works, offering an insight into their influential contributions to Greek literature.

Navagio Beach (Shipwreck Beach)

Zakynthos Island, Known for its striking beauty and the shipwreck that lies on its shores, Navagio Beach is one of Zakynthos' most iconic spots. Accessible only by boat, it offers visitors breathtaking views and an unforgettable experience.

play, making it an excellent location for a laid-back day by the sea.

Laganas Nature Park : Laganas, Zakynthos. Dedicated to preserving the loggerhead sea turtles (Caretta-Caretta), Laganas Nature Park offers stunning coastal views, hiking trails, and eco-friendly activities like bird watching, making it an ideal spot for nature lovers.

Top Beaches

Porto Limnionas Beach : Zakynthou-Keriou, Zakynthos, Ionian Islands, 29092, Set in a secluded cove surrounded by striking cliffs, Porto Limnionas is known for its crystal-clear waters, ideal for swimming, snorkeling, and diving. Its quiet location makes it a perfect spot for a relaxing day away from the crowds.

Gerakas Beach : 18 km south of Zakynthos Town, Gerakas Beach is famous for its soft, golden sand and clear waters, making it a great choice for families and nature enthusiasts

Banana Beach : 14 km southeast of Zakynthos Town, With its expansive golden sandy shoreline and inviting waters, Banana

Beach is well-equipped with snack bars, sun loungers, and watersports activities. It's a popular and lively destination, perfect for a day of fun and relaxation.

Xigia Beach : Zakynthos Island. A hidden treasure, Xigia Beach stands out for its untouched beauty and clear waters. It's an excellent location for snorkeling and appreciating the peaceful surroundings.

Agios Sostis Beach : Laganas Bay, Zakynthos,Accessible via a wooden bridge from Laganas Beach, Agios Sostis offers a tranquil escape with its scenic beach and crystal-clear waters. It's an idyllic place for a quiet retreat.

Interacting with Locals

Warm and Friendly Approach : A smile and a warm greeting go a long way when meeting locals. Saying "Yassas" (hello) or "Kalimera" (good morning) is a common and appreciated way to begin a conversation. Being friendly and respectful of local customs will help foster a positive interaction.

Learn Key Greek Words : While many people in Zakynthos speak English, learning a few basic Greek words will make your interactions more meaningful. Words like "Efharisto" (thank you), "Parakalo" (please), and "Signomi" (sorry) can help break the ice and show appreciation for the local language.

Respecting Local Customs: Zakynthos is rich in cultural traditions, so it's important to be mindful of local customs. Respect religious practices, dress modestly when entering churches, and participate in local festivals or events if invited it's a way to honor the island's heritage.

Dining Practices : In Zakynthos, sharing meals is an integral part of the social experience. Wait until everyone is served before you start eating, and don't be surprised if you're encouraged to share dishes. If invited to someone's home, it's a kind gesture to bring a small gift such as sweets or wine as a token of appreciation.

Engaging with Locals : The people of Zakynthos are known for their hospitality. Don't hesitate to strike up a conversation, ask for recommendations, or simply show interest in their culture and history. Locals will appreciate your genuine curiosity, and it's a great way to connect and enrich your travel experience.

NIGHTLIFE AND ENTERTAINMENT
Clubs And Bars

Club Zante Plaza : Laganas, Laganas, 29100, A favorite spot near Laganas Beach, Club Zante Plaza is known for its vibrant atmosphere, music, and dancing. It's a great venue for those looking to enjoy a night out with an excellent drink selection.

CherryBay : Laganas Main Street 881, Laganas, 290 92, A well-established name in Zakynthos nightlife, CherryBay has been a central hub for partygoers for over 30 years.

Cheeky Tikis Bar: Main Road, Zante, 29092. Known for its vibrant tiki-themed décor and creative cocktails, Cheeky Tikis Bar is a fun place to enjoy unique drinks and an energetic nightlife vibe in Laganas.

Breeze Bar : Tsilivi main road, Zakynthos, Tsilivi (Planos), 29100. Located within the Lazaros Hotel & Apartments complex, Breeze Bar offers a relaxed and family-friendly environment.

performances and themed nights, making it a great choice for families seeking entertainment.. Tsilivi, Zakynthos

Evening Entertainment

Infinity Beach Club Zante : Laganas Beach, Zakynthos, With a modern, minimalist design, Infinity Beach Club Zante creates a laid-back vibe ideal for an evening out. Enjoy live music, cocktails curated by an award-winning mixologist, and a stunning, photogenic setting.

Fantasy Mini Golf : Tsilivi, Zakynthos, Offering a fun, family-friendly experience, Fantasy Mini Golf features a variety of challenging courses set in beautifully landscaped surroundings perfect for an entertaining evening with loved ones.

Cheeky Tikis Bar : Main Road, Laganas, Zakynthos. Known for its quirky tiki-themed décor and unique cocktails, Cheeky Tikis Bar is a lively and vibrant spot for a night out with friends.

Portofino Cocktail Bar : Krioneri Road, Al. Merkati, Zakynthos. This cocktail bar offers stunning views of the Ionian Sea and the sparkling city lights. It's an excellent spot for a tranquil evening with refreshing drinks and a picturesque setting.

Tips For A Safe And Fun Night Out

Plan Ahead : Organize your night before heading out. Choose your destinations, have the addresses handy, and let someone know your plans. It's always better to be prepared.

Stay Hydrated and Eat Well : Drink water and have a good meal before you go out. This helps maintain your energy and lessens the impact of alcohol, ensuring a more enjoyable night.

Stick Together : If you're out with friends, stay close and look out for each other. It's safer and more fun to share the experience together.

Use Reliable Transportation : If you plan to drink, avoid driving. Pre-arrange a safe transportation method like a taxi or ride-sharing service to ensure a hassle-free return.

Be Respectful and Mindful : Respect local customs and traditions. Keep noise levels in check and behave thoughtfully so everyone can enjoy the night without disruptions.

OUTDOOR ACTIVITIES AND ADVENTURES

Boat Trips

Porto Vromi Maries Cruises & Fun

Zakynthos, Ionian Islands, 29100, Around €50 per person, 4-5 hours, This boat trip takes you to the iconic Shipwreck Beach (Navagio Beach) and the breathtaking sea caves of Zakynthos. With experienced captains ensuring a smooth ride, you'll even get a chance to stop on the beach, so there's no need to swim to get there.

Golden Dolphin Cruises

Zakynthos, Ionian Islands, 29100, Around €60 per person, 5-6 hours, Golden Dolphin offers various excursions, including island-wide tours, turtle watching, and a visit to Shipwreck Beach, the Blue Caves, and Xigia. With over 30 years of expertise, they promise an enriching and unforgettable journey.

Blue Shore Private Cruises

Tsilivi, Zakynthos, Ionian Islands, 29100, Customizable based on route and services, 3-6 hours, Blue Shore specializes in tailored boat tours, giving you the freedom to craft your own itinerary. You can visit famous spots like Shipwreck Beach, Blue Caves, Turtle Island, and private coves, all while enjoying a personalized experience with a skipper and tour guide.

Luxury Travel Zakynthos

Planos, Zakynthos, Ionian Islands, 29100, Around €100 per person, 6-8 hours, Offering a VIP experience, Luxury Travel Zakynthos provides spacious boats, snorkeling gear, and underwater cameras for an upscale adventure.

Zante Motorboat Rentals

Zakynthos, Ionian Islands, 29100, Customizable based on rental duration and services, Customizable, With Zante Motorboat Rentals, you can take control of your boat trip and explore at your own pace.

BLUE SHORE PRIVATE CRUISES

Tsilivi, Zakynthos, Ionian Islands, 29100. Blue Shore Private Cruises offers customized tours with a skipper and guide. Discover the island's stunning coastline while enjoying activities like snorkeling and diving.

LUXURY TRAVEL ZAKYNTHOS

Planos, Zakynthos, Ionian Islands, 29100, Providing a VIP experience, Luxury Travel Zakynthos offers spacious boats, snorkeling gear, and underwater cameras. The personalized service ensures a luxurious and unforgettable day on the water.

Blue Caves Exploration

Agios Nikolaos Port : Agios Nikolaos Port serves as the starting point for many boat tours to the Blue Caves. This charming harbor offers various boat options for exploring the caves and nearby attractions, making it an excellent place to begin your adventure.. Agios Nikolaos, Zakynthos, Ionian Islands, 29100

Skinari Lighthouse : Situated at the northernmost point of Zakynthos, Skinari Lighthouse provides breathtaking panoramic views of the Ionian Sea and surrounding landscapes. It's a scenic spot to visit before or after your Blue Caves tour. Skinari, Zakynthos, Ionian Islands, 29100

Mikro Nisi : Mikro Nisi is a small islet near the Blue Caves, famous for its crystal-clear waters and picturesque surroundings. It's a peaceful destination for snorkeling and unwinding after a boat trip, Mikro Nisi, Zakynthos, Ionian Islands, 29100

Makris Gialos Beach : Located close to the Blue Caves, Makris Gialos Beach features pristine waters, a sandy shoreline, and stunning views. It's perfect for swimming, snorkeling, and enjoying the sun. Makris Gialos, Zakynthos, Ionian Islands, 29100

Turtle Spotting

Gerakas Beach : A protected area and a key nesting site for loggerhead sea turtles, Gerakas Beach features soft golden sand and clear waters, making it a perfect location for spotting these magnificent creatures.. Gerakas, Zakynthos, Ionian Islands, 29100

Dafni Beach : Part of the National Marine Park of Zakynthos, Dafni Beach is renowned for its rich marine life and crystal-clear waters. It's an excellent spot for observing turtles, especially during the nesting season. Dafni, Zakynthos, Ionian Islands, 29100

Kalamaki Beach : Kalamaki Beach is a vital nesting ground for loggerhead sea turtles and forms part of the Zakynthos Marine Park. It offers a wonderful chance to see turtles in their natural habitat. Kalamaki, Zakynthos, Ionian Islands, 29100

Tsivili Beach : With clear waters and a sandy coastline, Tsivili Beach provides a peaceful environment to relax and spot turtles swimming in the shallow waters. Tsivili, Zakynthos, Ionian Islands, 29100

Porto Limnionas Swimming

Porto Limnionas is a beautiful and tranquil cove with crystal-clear waters, surrounded by towering cliffs. It offers an unforgettable swimming experience in its secluded setting. Here are the highlights:

- ➢ Address: Porto Limnionas, Agios Leon, Zakynthos, Ionian Islands, 29100, Greece

Crystal-Clear Waters: The waters are incredibly clear, providing excellent visibility for snorkeling and swimming. You can enjoy the beauty of the underwater rock formations and marine life in this pristine environment.

Secluded Cove: Though Porto Limnionas is a popular spot, it still retains a sense of being a hidden gem. The secluded location adds to its charm, offering visitors a peaceful escape.

Jumping Off Rocks: For the adventurous, Porto Limnionas offers natural rock platforms from which you can jump into the water. It's an exciting experience, but be sure to check the area for safety first.

Sunbathing and Relaxation: After swimming, you can unwind on the sunbeds or enjoy the shaded terrace of the local tavern.

variety of fruits, vegetables, herbs, and local specialties straight from the farmers. Near the entrance of Zakynthos Port, just behind the port authority.

SOLOMOS SQUARE : A lively square in Zakynthos Town that blends traditional and modern shopping. It's home to clothing stores, souvenir shops, and artisan products. Solomos Square, Zakynthos Town.

AGIOS MARKOS SQUARE : Another vibrant square in Zakynthos Town, featuring a wide range of shops selling everything from traditional Greek clothing to contemporary fashion. It's an excellent spot for unique gifts. Agios Markos Square, Zakynthos Town.

ADAIMEION CERAMIC ART STUDIO : A modern studio showcasing beautifully crafted ceramic art. It's the perfect place to find handmade gifts and decorative items. Adaimeion Ceramic Art Studio, Zakynthos Town.

Luxury Boutique And Malls

Abito Boutique : Abito Boutique offers a selection of upscale fashion, including clothing, accessories, and jewelry., Leonida Zoi 5, Zakynthos, Ionian Islands, 29100

Isola Boutique (Womenswear) : Specializing in women's fashion, Isola Boutique features a collection of stylish clothing and accessories. Arch. Episkopou, Lata 20, Zakynthos, Ionian Islands, 29100

Lynne : A well-established boutique since 1994, Lynne offers a variety of women's clothing and accessories.. Alexandrou Roma 89, Zakynthos, Ionian Islands, 29100

Black Pearl Boutique : Black Pearl Boutique is known for its luxury selection of fashion items, including clothing and accessories. Foskolou 16, Zakynthos, Ionian Islands, 29100

Zakynthos Shopping Mall : Located in the heart of Zakynthos Town, the Zakynthos Shopping Mall features a range of shops, including luxury brands and fashion retailers. Zakynthos Town Center, Zakynthos, Ionian Islands, 29100

Spa And Wellness Retreats

Majestic Hotel & Spa : Situated in Laganas, this spa offers an array of treatments, including massages and beauty services. It's an ideal spot for relaxation and rejuvenation.. Laganas Main Street, Laganas, 29092

ZanteZest : ZanteZest provides a holistic wellness experience with detox programs, yoga, Tai Chi, and healthy cooking classes. It's perfect for those looking to refresh both body and mind., Alykez, Zante, 29100

Porto Zante Villas & Spa : This luxury retreat offers over 20 spa treatments inspired by Greek nature and aromatherapy. It's a serene escape with a private waterfront spa.. Porto Zante Villas & Spa, Zakynthos, Ionian Islands, 29100

Holistic Heaven : Renowned for its exceptional massages and holistic treatments, Holistic Heaven offers a peaceful environment for ultimate relaxation and well-being. Zakynthos, Ionian Islands, 29100

Traditional Healing And Massage

Holistic Heaven : Holistic Heaven offers a variety of holistic treatments, including aromatherapy massage, hot stone massage, reiki, and reflexology. The focus is on healing clients mentally, physically, and spiritually. Porta Del Mar Beach Villas, Psarou Beach, Psarou, 29100

La Femme Spa : La Femme Spa provides a range of massage therapies, including full-body relaxing massage, leg & foot massage, head, neck, and shoulder massage, and deep tissue massage. Zakynthos, Ionian Islands, 29100

Majestic Hotel & Spa : Located in Laganas, Majestic Hotel & Spa offers a variety of treatments, including massages and beauty services. It's the perfect place to unwind and rejuvenate. Laganas Main Street, Laganas, 29092

Relax Spa & Beauty : Relax Spa & Beauty offers a range of massage therapies and beauty treatments in a serene environment, promoting relaxation and wellness. Zakynthos, Ionian Islands, 29100

Tips for Shopping Responsibly

Support Local Businesses : Purchasing from local businesses helps reduce the environmental impact of transportation and supports the local economy. Look for handmade, locally

Afternoon: Embark on a snorkeling excursion to Marathonisi (Turtle Island). The crystal-clear waters are ideal for exploring the vibrant marine life.

Evening: Relax at your accommodation or indulge in a leisurely beachside dinner.

Day 3: Watersport Adventures

Morning: Visit Porto Limnionas for a refreshing swim and some cliff diving. The sparkling waters are perfect for an adventurous dip.

Afternoon: Enjoy some kayaking or stand-up paddleboarding at Tsivili Beach, offering an exciting way to explore the coastline.

Evening: Savor a beachside barbecue or enjoy dinner at a nearby tavern.

Day 4: Final Relaxation and Departure

Morning: Spend a peaceful morning at Gerakas Beach, soaking in the soft golden sands and clear waters.

Afternoon: Head to Kalamaki Beach for some final moments of relaxation and fun beach activities.

Evening: Prepare for your departure while reflecting on your amazing beach and watersports adventure in Zakynthos.

7 Days Family Friendly Itinerary

Day 1: Arrival and Discovering Zakynthos Town

- ➢ Morning: Arrive in Zakynthos and settle into your accommodation.
- ➢ Afternoon: Take a stroll through Zakynthos Town, visiting landmarks like the Solomos Museum and the Venetian Port.
- ➢ Evening: Enjoy a family dinner at Remezzo, a local favorite.

Day 2: A Day at Laganas Beach

- ➢ Morning: Start the day with breakfast at The Sizzler.
- ➢ Afternoon: Head to Laganas Beach for a relaxing day of sunbathing and swimming.
- ➢ Evening: Enjoy a delicious dinner at Zorbas Tavern.

Day 3: Boat Trip to Navagio Beach

- ➢ Morning: Have breakfast at your hotel.

- Afternoon: Take a boat trip to the iconic Navagio Beach (Shipwreck Cove).
- Evening: Return to Zakynthos Town and enjoy a dinner at a local restaurant.

Day 4: Turtle Watching and Snorkeling Adventure

- Morning: Visit Laganas Bay for an exciting turtle spotting experience.
- Afternoon: Embark on a snorkeling trip to Marathonisi (Turtle Island).
- Evening: Unwind at your accommodation or dine at a beachside restaurant.

Day 5: Watersports Fun

- Morning: Visit Porto Limnionas for cliff diving and a swim in the clear waters.
- Afternoon: Try out kayaking or stand-up paddleboarding at Tsivili Beach.
- Evening: Enjoy a meal at a local tavern.

Day 6: Beach Relaxation and Souvenir Shopping

- Morning: Spend a relaxing morning at Gerakas Beach.

- ➢ Afternoon: Browse local shops in Laganas for unique souvenirs.
- ➢ Evening: Have dinner at a charming beachside restaurant.

Day 7: Departure and Final Exploration

- ➢ Morning: Enjoy your last morning at Kalamaki Beach.
- ➢ Afternoon: Pack up and get ready for your departure.
- ➢ Evening: Reflect on your wonderful trip and enjoy one final meal in Zakynthos Town.

5 Days Curlinary Itenarary

Day 1: Arrival and Traditional Greek Dining

Morning: Arrive in Zakynthos and settle into your accommodation.

Afternoon: Explore Zakynthos Town and visit the local market to immerse yourself in the island's fresh produce.

Dinner: Enjoy a traditional Greek meal at Taverna To Steki in Zakynthos Town, where you can savor classic dishes like moussaka, souvlaki, and fresh seafood.

Address: Lomvardou 3, Zakynthos, Ionian Islands, 29100

Dinner: Savor an organic seafood dinner at Nobelos Bio Restaurant in Agios Nikolaos, known for its fresh, sustainable dishes.

Address: Agios Nikolaos, Zakynthos, Ionian Islands, 29100

Day 5: Departure and Last Meal

Morning: Start your day with a delicious breakfast at Gusto in Zakynthos Town, renowned for its pastries and coffee.

Address: Lomvardou 2, Zakynthos, Ionian Islands, 29100

Afternoon: Take a final stroll around Zakynthos Town, picking up any last-minute souvenirs.

Lunch: Enjoy a final Greek meal at Ammos Taverna in Laganas, where you can sample a variety of traditional dishes.

Address: Laganas, Zakynthos, Ionian Islands, 29100

Evening: Reflect on your delicious journey through Zakynthos as you prepare for your departure.

CONCLUSION

Congratulations! You've made it to the end of this Zakynthos Travel Guide, and hopefully, you've gathered all the essential tips, exciting itineraries, and local insights you need to make the most of your time on this beautiful island. As you reflect on the many experiences that await you in Zakynthos—from its iconic beaches and crystal-clear waters to its vibrant culture and delicious cuisine we hope you're filled with excitement for the adventures ahead.

Zakynthos is more than just a destination; it's a place where the stunning landscapes, rich history, and warm hospitality come together to create lasting memories. Whether you're planning to explore the peaceful shores of Gerakas, spot sea turtles in Laganas Bay, or discover the secrets of Navagio Beach, this island promises something for every kind of traveler. Perhaps you'll unwind with a quiet afternoon at a local taverna, savoring the flavors of freshly prepared Greek dishes, or venture out on the water to try your hand at watersports and discover hidden coves along the coastline.

But beyond the sightseeing and adventures, it's the spirit of Zakynthos that will stay with you. From the locals who greet you with a warm smile to the serene landscapes that invite you to pause and take in the beauty of the moment, Zakynthos has a way of making you feel at home. So, as you embark on your journey, remember to take your time, embrace the island's laid-back pace, and make space for spontaneous discoveries that will make your trip truly special. As you set off to explore the wonders of Zakynthos, we hope this guide has helped you craft the perfect itinerary, filled with experiences that are meaningful to you. Whether it's a relaxing day at the beach, a thrilling watersport adventure, or a culinary feast at a local taverna, there's no wrong way to enjoy this incredible island.

Thank you for choosing this guide as your companion to Zakynthos. May your trip be filled with unforgettable moments, new friendships, and stories to share for years to come. Safe travels, and we hope you'll carry a piece of Zakynthos with you, wherever you go.

Until we meet again, happy travels!